SCENES FROM
AN ALLOTMENT GARDEN

Scenes from an Allotment Garden

Betty Emmaline Walker

William Sessions Limited
York, England

ISBN 1 85072 286 2

Also by the same author
The Green Lanes, A Westmorland Childhood

Printed in 10 on 12 point Palatino typeface
from Author's disk
by Sessions of York, The Ebor Press,
York YO31 9HS
England

CONTENTS

for L.

sine qua non

PROLOGUE

It all began in the middle of July on the day I returned home from Paris.

I had been on holiday with my son 'doing' the Galleries and Museums, and my mind was still very much occupied with the art treasures I had seen and with the buildings and the atmosphere of that great city. We had parted company in Manchester, he to his home in the Pennines, I, eastward to the plains.

My husband, L., met me at the station and after enquiring briefly about the state of my health and if I had enjoyed my holiday, he launched into the subject uppermost in his mind as we drove to the village where we lived. "I want you to look at an allotment", he said. "I have taken it provisionally - it has two sheds on it". "Ah", I thought, "two sheds. What plans has he in mind for two sheds?" My thoughts were anything but organised and my mind was in something of a turmoil as I tried to assimilate what L. was saying as he warmed to his subject. After all I had just returned from a cultural holiday in France, and still in the forefront of my mind were the Monet paintings at the Quai D'Orsay and in the Orangerie, and here I was confronted immediately on my return with the idea of taking on an allotment garden - not in a few weeks' time when I would have had time to think about it and perhaps get used to the idea before making up my mind; a decision was needed now. This very afternoon.

One half of me thought that with my house and garden to look after I had quite enough to do at my time of life, but the other half of me was really quite keen and excited at the prospect. Thoughts of a quiet retirement for myself in the near future began to slip away as I was swept along by L's enthusiasm. I had lived for so many years without a real garden, and here was the opportunity to get to grips with one.

Thus with my mind in a whirl we reached our home. *Paris et ses Merveilles* (Paris and her Marvels) were put on one side as I quickly prepared a snack lunch; my old diaries, to which I shall refer from time to time, tell me that this

1

consisted of poached eggs on toast. We sat for a while and rested as L. expounded on his plans for the garden (and for the sheds), and after changing into our working attire we cycled to the allotment field, a distance of about a quarter-of-a-mile.

There were three different approaches to the gardens. The route which we took that day was along the public highway to a gate on the left-hand side of the road and immediately before a bridge, which had until fairly recently been over the railway. Due to re-routing the railway line this part of the track was no longer used and had been converted into a cycle path which ran along one side of the allotment field. We paused at the gate before opening it and looked across the plots. The gardens were on a lower level than the road and so we had an excellent view over the whole allotment field.

The area we were looking at covered about three-and-a-half acres. From this first sight of the gardens it appeared that almost all the plots were under cultivation and thick with crops, not surprisingly as this was the height of the season. Looking from the gate we could see rows of tall broad bean plants, potatoes, peas, feathery carrot tops, waving sweet corn, onions and salad crops.

We released the bolt on the gate and as it swung open inwards we trundled down the slope and along the grassy path, tidy plots of well-ordered greenery on either side. Now we could see that the bean and pea pods were ready for picking. There were signs that some potatoes had already been dug. Different varieties of lettuce were interspersed with Spring onions and radishes, and amongst it all were the fruit bushes. Would we ever grow crops like these, I wondered, as we cycled slowly along the green path and past a motley assortment of interesting-looking sheds.

After about a hundred yards along the green path we reached a shed. The shed boasted a corrugated roof covered in brambles and with nettles and thistles growing up the walls. Next to it was a broken-down Nissen hut, open at both ends. We leaned our bikes against the hut, for this was indeed Number Twenty, the vacant plot with two sheds on it.

PROLOGUE

*   *   *

I gazed down the plot to the hedge in the distance. Through long grass I could see raspberry canes and red currant bushes, their branches heavy with fruit; gooseberry bushes where the fruit was almost too ripe and turning pink; laden blackcurrant bushes where the fruit would soon be ripening, and beyond them what looked like a field of waving grass, thistles and nettles, so tall that I almost disappeared from view when I walked into it. Here were great clumps of rhubarb, some going to seed, and brambles with flowers like wild roses.

I do not think that I ever considered refusing to take it on. I might have done so had it not been for the soft fruit. It occurred to me straightaway that it would be horsework to clear even a few yards of the weed-infested ground for cultivation. The nettles and couch grass with their running underground stems and roots were never likely to be completely eradicated. But that first afternoon when we had completed the formalities of rental ('rent free for the first six months') we returned there to survey what was now our plot, and took with us two containers to fill with raspberries and gooseberries.

From that moment of dropping the rasps into the basin (and into my mouth), I was hooked. The whole incomparable scent and taste of summer was for me embodied in those first minutes of fruit-picking. I saw the opportunity here offered to escape from the telephone and the doorbell and the myriad other household tasks and duties. With this in mind the problems of perennial weeds loomed nothing like so large, and were thrust, temporarily, into the background.

In the immediately following period the barometer was *Set Fair* and the temperature was up to eighty degrees fahrenheit, much too warm for the sort of heavy work we were starting - fixing posts to fasten up the first row of raspberry canes. We had agonised that first evening over what was the most urgent job to tackle. Should we start at once to clear a patch of ground for sowing and planting? This would take some time, and meanwhile the unsupported raspberry canes were in immediate need of attention, being,

3

as they were, heavy with fruit. So we took with us next day an assortment of tools, a bottle of orange juice to refresh us and a packet of paper hankies to cope with my hay fever. As L. hammered in the posts and strung wire between them, I cleared away the grass and thistles from around the canes: the need to sit down and rest during this activity very soon became apparent.

Having completed the knocking in of the posts and fastening the canes to the wire L. set about making a seat. The uprights of a previous seat were already in position and it was not long before we were actually sitting on the 'new' seat, a stout plank from L's wood store at home, securely fastened to the uprights. That, we felt, was enough for the second day of our tenancy. However, after a meal, and fortified by the products of the garden and of the recent holiday in France (and here my diary tells me that we consumed raspberries, Boursin cheese and crackers and *vin rouge*), we were ready to go again, if only to survey our handiwork and to pick more soft fruit to make into puddings and pies.

Our friends and neighbours - and indeed our fellow plotholders - must have had reservations about our sanity, taking on six-hundred-and-sixty square yards of untended and neglected allotment garden at our time of life, though they were considerate enough not to say so. L was then sixty-eight and I was almost sixty and just about to retire from what had become a loss-making hobby of selling bric-a-brac and curios from a little shop on the outskirts of the nearby city. In fact one man remarked that at our age we should be giving up allotment gardening instead of just starting it.

Here we could have pointed out that as far as we could see most of the plotholders were retired men (although they no doubt had been gardening there for years already). So we were not deterred by this observation, in fact it strengthened our resolve, because the idea of growing our own fruit and vegetables was not a new one - it had been in the back of our minds for years but until now we had never had the time to do it. It was therefore a project for our, and more especially for my, retirement. Little did we know then how it would dominate and take over our very lives.

CHAPTER ONE

We were not complete strangers to allotment gardening. In the mid- to late-1940s, as newly-weds, we had rented a small allotment in another group of gardens in the area of the city where we were then living. We had grown potatoes, cabbages and some salad crops, the cultivation of which was fairly simple. It was not very successful mainly because we were both working full time, had few tools, no access to manure and no money to spare to buy fertilisers or pest controls, even if these had been available. But at that time everything was in short supply and almost all foodstuffs were rationed.

In fact post-War food shortages were more acute than they had been during the War years. The egg allowance for example was one egg per person per week, and great was the deliberation as to how and when this egg should be eaten, or even if it should be put into making a cake, together with the margarine and sugar ration for the week. L. being a manual worker qualified for extra sugar and cheese, and for extra bread (bread was rationed for a time). Coupons for bread - called Bread Units - were known as BU's and this abbreviation caused some vulgarity and mirth, though it was no joke if you had used up all your BU's for the week and did not know where the next loaf was coming from at the week-end.

We bought bread at a little corner shop which sold a variety of goods. The owner of the shop was a large lady called Annie who would tell me from time to time, when there was a lull in custom, of her "big body operation" - a euphemism for a hysterectomy (an unmentionable word in those days), and how she was lucky to have survived it. She was very much the boss over her quiet and meek husband Charlie. When we were short of bread and had no BU's left on a Saturday evening I could almost always count on a loaf from Charlie (without BU's) - but before producing one he invariably said, "I'll have to go and ask *Her*", and indeed disappeared through to the back-shop to be given permission to sell me an 'under-the-counter' loaf, though the sympathetic expression on his face clearly said, "I would sell *you* a loaf without BU's at any time".

And so the few vegetables we grew on our allotment were a valuable and important addition to our diet. This was further augmented by our growing of tomatoes. As tenants of a ground-floor flat we had the use of the long narrow garden at the back of the Victorian terrace house which was our first home. Here L. erected a small lean-to greenhouse, put together from scrap wood, glass and bricks which he either bought very cheaply or negotiated to acquire by barter or some other (entirely legal) means from an acquaintance who dealt in such commodities. When I think about it this may well have been the beginning of his predilection for sheds and outbuildings.

About two years later we moved to another district of the city to take over a sweets-and-tobacco shop and as a consequence had to give up the allotment. There was no proper garden at the new address, though there was a long open piece of land behind our property where several tiny cottages had once stood and which had recently been demolished. The area looked untidy; however the exigencies of the business we had acquired made it impracticable to transform what looked like a bombed-site into a garden - but it might be just the place to keep a few hens.

We bought a white Wyandot hen which we called Daisy, and several richly-coloured Anconas. What we did not know then was that Anconas were a type of game bird. They nested in the ivy-clad wall instead of in the hen hut we had provided, and flew off and laid most of their eggs elsewhere. Perhaps we should have clipped their wings - but that operation was beyond our knowledge at the time, or our capabilities.

Keeping hens meant that the egg ration had to be surrendered to buy hen food - a type of meal which we boiled up in a pan on the kitchen fire and which smelled like unappetising porridge. I suppose the wayward hens produced more than two eggs a week for us, and therefore more than the official egg ration, but keeping hens turned out to be a frustrating occupation and one which we soon abandoned.

It came about that with one thing and another successful allotment gardening was to be consigned to day-dreams for the next forty years. Surely, you will think, they had time - sometime during those four decades - to take on another allotment? But no; the fact was that our work, always self-employed - and our family - were so demanding that gardening, even on a moderate scale, was out of the question.

But here we were at last, L. retired and I on the verge of it, about to embark on a project of which we knew really very little. We would no doubt make mistakes, but we would be ready to listen to those with experience and to learn from them. We were full of enthusiasm for this new venture, but even in those early days the body was not quite as willing as the spirit.

CHAPTER TWO

We had decided to call our plot 'the Croft'. The Nissen hut became 'the Black House'. These assigned names reminded us of the traditional descriptions of home and land in the Isle of Skye where we had spent summer holidays over the previous twenty years. No time now even to think of holidays, past, present or future; our minds became firmly fixed on one track, that being the path which led to the Allotment field.

We already had a nodding acquaintance around the village with several plotholders. We soon got to know others: Matt, Tommy, Taffy, Ernest, Brian and Sylvia, Nick and Marilyn, and Llew. Our next-but-one allotment neighbour brought us strawberries from his plot, and we gave him raspberries from ours. Very soon gifts of spring onions, lettuce and beetroot appeared at the Black House door. At first we were rather taken aback by this unexpected generosity so early in our tenancy, and from people we hardly knew. But we soon discovered that this giving of produce was normal practice. Most plotholders grew too much for their own needs, though not all crops turned out successfully. Those which did were handed round, and so an exchange system became a matter of course and everyone benefited. It would be some time before we had surplus vegetables, but in the meantime there was the soft fruit which we could offer.

The making of the seat, and the setting upright of the Nissen hut and making it weatherproof, rather amused our fellow gardeners. They saw at once that our priorities were to provide a place to rest and a hut which would shelter us and our tools when it rained. Their first remarks were, 'you've got a job on there', and Llew even went so far as to say to L. that the garden would keep him out of mischief, which was Llew's way of saying that it would keep him occupied in his retirement. What Llew did not know was that L. never had time on his hands. His many interests and hobbies and the maintenance of the house and garden made one wonder what, amongst these activities, would become neglected in order to work the allotment. Our fellow plotholders knew only too well the enormity of the task we had set ourselves. But they were never intrusive; they let us get on with it even though they were understandably curious over the restoration of the Black House, and they were genuine in their praise of L's expertise.

Matt, whose plot was across the green path from ours, was obviously very interested in our activities though he had said little except to show concern as to whether I would injure myself when I was tackling the cutting down of waist-high nettles around the redcurrant bushes. I soon learned that he was the most experienced gardener on the Allotment field and had followed his father who had had a plot there for thirty years. In fact Matt's first encounters with the allotments had been the occasions when his mother pushed him down there in his pram.

Now one read the gardening books and then asked Matt if what the book said was correct. One fellow gardener had said of Matt, "if he sees that you are really interested he will help you". (This advice happened to come from a man whose chief gardening aim seemed to be growing outdoor strawberries in the summer, freezing them and eating them on Christmas Day.) The truth of this report was soon borne out when after a word with L. Matt began to scythe the weeds on our plot, and gave us two very good forks without shafts as well. L. soon fitted shafts onto them and painted mine, a ladies' fork, bright red. When I showed it to Matt he asked if it had become red-hot with so much use.

There was soon plenty of rubbish, and the obvious way to dispose of it was to burn it and so we had a bonfire in the middle of the plot. One thing led to another and having seen the effects of the fire on the weeds which were still growing we decided to hire a flame-throwing weed burner. This was a ferocious piece of equipment which gobbled up the fuel at an alarming rate and soon had us feeling pretty hot ourselves. It produced results - albeit rather more slowly than we had hoped - but what with the hiring cost and the fuel cost it was going to be an expensive business, so after a day or two we decided that this project had to be abandoned.

CHAPTER TWO

Having scythed the bottom half of the plot - which we called 'the Field' - Matt turned his attention to the top half and to my great consternation chopped off all the rhubarb. "There'll be plenty of rhubarb", he said reassuringly; and of course there was, from his own crowns that year, and more than we could eat, freeze and give away every following season from our own. However some holiday caravanners in the area were accustomed to strolling into the Allotment field and asking of anyone who was about for "a bit of rhubarb", adding, "the wife likes a bit of rhubarb you know". Generous Matt had once said, "help yourself", which they did, pulling every stick from the plants. When these greedy people returned the following year and asked for "a bit of rhubarb", Matt informed them that his plants were 'resting' - as indeed some of them were (rhubarb growers habitually 'rest' a selected number of crowns each year especially those which have been 'forced' the previous year). They did not come again.

So what might we be able to grow so late in the season? Lettuce, radishes and spinach; yes, they would be alright, and someone gave us a handful of leek seedlings. We rushed to the book to find out how to deal with them, trimming the roots with scissors, making a hole with the dibber and dropping a seedling into each well-watered hole. Matt gave us a lecture on the dreaded club root which he said was prevalent all over the allotments, and showed us how it affected some of his brassicas. This sent us scurrying out to buy Calomel dust to scatter among the Brussels sprouts, purple sprouting broccoli and January King Cabbage plants. Whatever precautions we took over the years we lost most of our brassica crops due to club root. The book said, "where there is club root do not grow brassicas for twenty years". Well, we could not wait that long so we kept trying, but all we managed were a few summer cabbages.

CHAPTER THREE

L had finished the restoration of the Black House and put up some shelves for small tools, bottles, tins and boxes. Plenty of room on the floor for our forks, spades, rakes, buckets and all the paraphernalia indispensible to allotment gardening, which we very soon collected together.

The other shed was a very stout building. It had been constructed and used originally for keeping pigs; one half the pig-run and the other half the pig-sty. L. re-roofed the pig-sty and built up the walls of the pig-run and put a roof on that. We retained the name of the pig-sty - what we used it for will be revealed later - and the pig-run became the Summer House where we planned to sit in our chairs and to brew and dispense tea (made on either a primus or a Calor gas stove) to all comers. No time for that at present however.

I was busy making a herb garden around the sheds when Llew strolled over, the ever-present cigarette in his fingers. "Ye'll be ninety-two before ye've finished", said he. Not much encouragement there but no difficulty getting the mint to grow. The only problem once it was established, Llew assured me, was preventing it from invading the whole plot. With this in mind we decided to contain it within a wide piece of broken drainpipe, and here it flourished.

Llew was a small, elderly man with a squarish head and wrinkled face. His dark hair was of rather greasy appearance and was brushed straight back. He had a lugubrious countenance and I do not think that I ever saw him smile, though he was not without a dry humour, and voiced his opinion loudly on a variety of topics.

On the Sunday mornings when we either walked or cycled to the eight o'clock Service at the Parish Church we passed Llew leaning on the wall at the Main-Street-end of the road where he lived, enjoying the early morning air, the quietness of the as-yet-unawakened village, and the first or maybe the second cigarette of the day. He and his wife attended Parish Evensong every Sunday, Llew looking

13

somewhat uncomfortable in his best suit and stiff white collar. During the Service he could clearly be heard making comments on the choir, the choice of hymns, the Bible readings and more particularly on the Vicar's text and the content and length of the sermon. These remarks were mainly addressed to his wife, who sat completely impassive as though she was either not with him or had not heard a word he uttered.

This lady, 'Mrs' Llew, ran a shop of sorts from her front sitting-room. She sold eggs, brought to her by a local farmer, and sub-standard chocolates known as 'mis-shapes' from the nearby chocolate factory. As a retired employee of the factory she was able, as a concession, to buy these chocolates very cheaply. In turn she sold the goods to people like myself - who did not mind a chocolate wafer biscuit which had been improperly wrapped or which had a slight dent in it - at a small profit to herself and cheaper than I could buy at the local shops. On the occasions when she was away from the house Llew 'looked after' the shop. He also had the daily task of preparing the vegetables for the midday dinner. If I happened to call for eggs or chocolates late in the morning Llew would be standing in front of the sink, not upright but leaning both his forearms on it - with his back bent - peeling potatoes or cutting up the greens. Now retired, his working life had been spent mainly on farms at various labouring jobs, and on pay-day he handed over his unopened wage packet to his wife (so she told me) and from it she gave him his 'pocket money' for the week. This was soon dissipated at one of the local public houses where he went every lunch-time for a pint of beer and a glass of rum, and from time to time to slip a Mars bar across the counter to the barmaid. And it was here that the landlord, after a refurbishment of the pub, fixed a brass plate to the area of the bar on which Llew habitually leaned, proclaiming that indeed this was 'Llew's Place'.

Selling chrysanthemums from his allotment and doing a bit of odd-job gardening - for example clipping the hedge around the churchyard and making wreaths at Christmas time and selling them (having first acquired the wire frames from the rubbish heap in the churchyard) - provided him with a bit of extra cash to pay for his lunch-time pleasures when his pocket-money had run out.

Having heeded Llew's warnings about the mint I next turned my attention and energies to compost-making. Here I had to rely on the book, as Matt - our usual guide and resort - did not appear to make compost. "Nine inches of vegetable waste and anything biodegradable, nine inches of farmyard manure, well rotted and sprinkled well with lime, nine inches of soil then start again with vegetable waste" - so ran the instructions. For the making of compost L. built two containers. He used a variety of otherwise unservice-able materials - old doors, corrugated tin, and wooden planks. Compost-making became an obsession with me, even to the extent of digging up worms and transferring them from the garden to the compost bin. "In six months", said the book, "the compost should be crumbly, just like a Christmas cake".

Even saving every scrap of vegetable waste from the kitchen I had precious little to build up into nine inches. There were, as yet, no surplus crops to shred up nor any which had bolted and gone to seed. There were however the grass mowings from the lawn at home and we even had a trip around the village gathering up fallen leaves later in the year. I covered it all up in wet weather and uncovered it in dry weather. We were fortunate in having a farmer nearby who would sell us manure by the cartload, and deliver it - and from time to time sacks of horse manure would appear, dumped just inside the gate and free for the barrowing. So there were no excuses for crops not growing.

Meanwhile Matt had cast his eye over the Field and pro-nounced it ready for weedkiller. One evening we observed that markers had been fixed to show what had been sprayed and what had not. His next task was to rotovate the the top half of the Field. This, he said, had been over-cultivated and recommended us to cultivate the bottom half; and to egg us on deposited Butterhead lettuces at the Black House door of such perfection that I was loath to take them to pieces to eat.

SCENES FROM AN ALLOTMENT GARDEN

We dug over and pulled out the 'wicks' from where we had rotovated and one of our younger neighbours remarked that we were 'like beavers'. What indeed were we doing to ourselves going to bed feeling half dead and aching from top to toe, and getting up in the morning still aching and stiff all over? I cooked mountains of fruit and vegetables but never had time even to flick a duster about in the house. From time to time the seemingly never-ending prospect of so much hard work depressed me and I wondered what we did before we started it all.

But we had passed the point of no return. Even if we had thought of backing out and quitting, which in fact we had not, we could never have lost face by giving it all up so soon, having already put so much work into it. And what about that £100 rotovator? The thought of how much fruit and vegetables could be bought in the shops for that sum had not escaped me.

In spite of the gruelling hard work, the aching limbs and the neglected domestic matters, the satisfaction we experienced in going down to the garden and getting to grips with the cultivation of the land was so immense that it outweighed all the difficulties. I, in particular, palpably relaxed the moment I cycled through the gate and along the green path. I turned the key in the padlock, threw open the Black House door, picked out my fork from amongst the clutter and sat on the seat for a few minutes to savour the quietness and the smell of the earth before beginning to work the soil.

It was at times like this that I felt particularly close to my father. Both my parents had been keen gardeners. My mother grew the flowers and my father grew the fruit and vegetables. In his quiet way he would so much have approved of what I was doing. He would have stood there, watching me at work, wearing his old tweed jacket, his corduroy trousers and his clogs, smoking his pipe. And from time to time he would have gently offered advice from his lifetime's experience; pleased to see that I was carrying on a family tradition - even in such a small way - of working on the land as our yeoman-farmer forebears had done. I often felt that his spirit was there with me encouraging me in what I was doing and urging me to continue.

CHAPTER FOUR

From the very beginning we seemed to need a vast amount of tools and equipment. We already had the basics in the form of a fork, a spade, a rake, a hoe, a pair of shears and a few hand tools. Our very elderly neighbour at home, a retired farmer's widow, invited us to help ourselves from her shed to tools now surplus to her requirements. As L. did all her odd jobs and helped her with one or two tasks in her garden we felt justified in taking up her offer. We thus acquired a cultivator, another hoe, another fork and spade and a very rusty six-pound hammer, indispensible for knocking in posts.

The gardening books and magazines which we read, constantly reminded us that gardening was a dangerous occupation - as indeed it can be. Holding posts upright while L. hammered them in with a sledge hammer was a nerve-racking experience but one from which I emerged unscathed on each occasion. Then if you were not brained by standing on the head of the rake you were quite likely to drive the prongs of a fork or the blade of the spade into your foot (if you were not concentrating on the job), not to mention the damage you could inflict on yourself with sharp knives, secateurs and shears. A tetanus injection seemed to be a sensible precaution and one which we took.

And not only implements were hazardous. Close encounters with some plants could make life quite uncomfortable. Treating stinging nettles and thistles with respect (and thick gloves) was obvious, but picking fruit - raspberries and particularly blackberries and gooseberries - could result in scratched and sore hands and arms if you did not wear long sleeves and occasionally gloves. Then there were the bugs. In warm late-summer weather pink lumps appeared on parts of the anatomy not normally on view, and could itch like mad for days (and nights), the bugs having penetrated the outer layer of clothing.

As I have said, Matt had given us two forks onto which L. had fitted shafts so we now had three forks, two spades and hoes, a rake and a cultivator, a pair of shears and a six-pound hammer. Rooting about in boxes in dark corners of L's workshop an ancient pair of secateurs came to light, a small pair of shears also, and even a pair of sheep-shears; (what were we doing with sheep-shears tucked away in an old Zebo black-lead box?). L. made a giant rake using six-inch nails for the prongs and this proved invaluable for raking up weeds after rotovating.

The provenance of other items we acquired was unusual to say the least. Beyond the hedge at the bottom of our plot was an old neglected orchard once belonging to the railway company and then British Railways and now owned by Sustrans, creators of the cycle track from the dis-used mainline railway. The orchard had once been rented from British Railways by a village eccentric known locally as Black Bob - 'black' because of his aversion to soap and water. He and his hens and other livestock all lived together in a bungalow in the village in somewhat unsavoury conditions. He accumulated anything and everything he could lay hands on and was never known to get rid of anything.

Black Bob also rented the allotment nearest to the road and kept poultry there as well as at home. Matt told us, with evident relish, that Bob had once slipped on the steep bank between the road and his plot and had fallen onto some of his hens. He put two of them and a cock-bird (apparently unharmed) into a bucket and took them home as pets.

Another tale which Matt related with even more relish was that of a local farmer, who was also a butcher, who used to bring Bob recently severed cows' heads - complete in every particular - for Bob to hang in the branches of a small tree near his plot so that his hens could fly up and peck them. It was not long before rats took to tree-climbing and helping themselves to a free meal. The stench from the rotting heads was quite something according to Matt.

After Bob's demise several old bicycles were removed from the bungalow - along with all the other detritus - onto the Corporation skip. The orchard wilderness, on our investigation, yielded up a carrier bicycle, two very rusty iron wheelbarrows and an excellent galvanised bath with two handles, all presumably dumped there by Bob when there was no more room at the bungalow.

A small cottage between us and the next village had recently been demolished, and poking about amongst the debris L. unearthed what on first appearance might have been, and certainly looked like, an implement from ancient Rome. Not impossible in view of the fact that the Romans inhabited this land from about AD 150, and that the Roman road from Eboracum to Deva (York to Chester) was only a few hundred yards away. It was in fact the business-end of a small hay fork encrusted with rust, pebbles and even shells. Cleaned up and fastened to the end of a shaft it became regularly employed lifting rubbish onto and into the fire container (an old galvanised dustbin of pre-Wheelie-Bin days) and thus sooted and blackened lost all trace of its former existence as an agricultural implement.

We did actually buy some new and second-hand equipment. It became evident quite early on that if we were to make any headway and keep on top of the work we needed a rotovator, particularly having seen Matt's in operation. We first borrowed one from a friend but found it hardly satisfactory and were relieved when he decided not to sell it. We scanned the advertisements in the local paper and before long found ourselves parting with the one-hundred pounds already alluded to for a very good second-hand 'Merry Tiller' which even L. said years later was worth every penny. Local firms selling agricultural machinery had a sale of garden tools and here we bought a new green plastic watering can, a new lightweight galvanised wheelbarrow and a pair of sheeps' toenail cutters at about a quarter of the price of identical secateurs. So, well equipped as we were with tools and machinery for every task, all we really had to do now was to get on with it.

CHAPTER FIVE

One of our immediate neighbours on half of the adjoining plot was an old man called Eddie. A retired small farmer and bachelor until late in life he had eventually married his housekeeper. A pale, cadaverous-looking man - his health was failing - his garden was his great interest and he came down regularly if only to stand and look at it, hands deep in his pockets. He was of that dying breed who put doctors, clergymen, army officers and other professionals on a pedestal and he supplied two of these retired men living nearby with free garden produce as though it was a privilege to do so.

One evening he came down to the garden in some distress; his cat had disappeared and his wife was quite distraught. "It's such a clever cat", he explained, "it opens the casement window to let itself out, and what's more if the phone rings when we are in bed it comes and paws our faces until we get up and answer it". A clever cat indeed. I became quite anxious myself about its disappearance and cycled a couple of miles south along the track looking for it. But no black cat to be seen. Then to the relief of all it turned up the following day, not quite clever enough however to say where it had been.

During that first cold winter on the few occasions when we went down to dig and to light a fire Eddie could be seen struggling with a spade digging five spadefuls and then having to rest and lean heavily on the spade. He was wearing an old overcoat and the flat cap which was a part of him - I never saw him without the cap so do not know whether he had hair or was bald. "Come and get warm Eddie", I called, and he came slowly over and stood at the fire, stretching out his arms and his gnarled old hands to the warmth, and savouring it.

After Eddie died his wife kept on the plot to pick the fruit and vegetables and to light fires and burn all manner of rubbish, mainly papers from the house. She had always been keen to light a fire on the plot and though she took no part in the cultivation of the land she (like many other wives) helped to harvest the crops. Some months after Eddie's death I went down to the Croft and saw Matt standing with his spade and looking, I thought, not quite himself. I went over to him and asked, "Hello Matt, are you alright?" "I've just buried Eddie's cat", he replied in rather a flat voice, "It got run over and Eddie's wife wanted it burying here".

A retired Major who had been on the receiving end of Eddie's produce turned up on one or two occasions after Eddie's wife had given up the plot and helped himself liberally to rhubarb. L. called out to him on one of these occasions, "There has been a lot of thieving from these allotments recently, if you're not careful people will think you're the culprit". He did not appear again. The two men who took over Eddie's garden both died within six months of one another. Word of these tragedies must have got around because no one else took it on. It had become the Doomed plot.

Near to the blackberry bushes, half-way down our own plot, there was a peculiar little hill of earth and stones. We decided to carry out a sort of archaeological dig on it. In the process we unearthed barrow-loads of sticks, stones, bricks, bits of old iron, string, wire, clay-pipe bowls and stems, bits of coloured pottery and even part of a tiny white pottery figure - the top half of a male clown or some such entertainer.

We pondered on the origins of these fragments. The clay-pipe stems and bowls would have come from generations of men who had smoked their pipes as they tended their allotments. Clay pipes were cheap. During the 1920s and 1930s they cost only one penny each but had a short life - the stems broke easily and if the pipe was dropped it would break into two or three pieces; it was not practical to repair it and as a replacement cost so little the broken pieces were left where they had fallen.

The shards of pottery were not so easily explained. We could only think that mugs or cups - brought to the gardens with a snack or a picnic - had been dropped from time to time, and with constant digging and rotovating of the soil had become fragmented. But the tiny pottery figure was more of a mystery and one to which there was no apparent answer.

There was an abundance of pottery pieces to be picked up in the nearby fields, particularly those fields near to where the railway line had been. They were regularly ploughed up by the farmers and we had on our walks collected up hundreds of such pieces, some bearing the lettering of former railway companies, the LMS and the LNER. We were always intending to make a collage with them, but like many other projects that idea had to be temporarily shelved. Had these items of crockery been dropped accidentally from the train windows or had they been deliberately hurled out? It was fascinating to speculate, but we had to get back to the job in hand.

When we levelled the ground L. made stout supports for the row of blackberry bushes, and in the middle of the row where there was a space he built an arch. We later discovered on reading some old gardening legends that walking through a blackberry arch was the panacea for all ills. It did not however seem to produce any beneficial effect on aching limbs.

By the end of our first year we had cleared most of the weeds, planted spring cabbages, leeks and purple-sprouting broccoli and sown Aquadulce broad beans. L. had made a seat, restored the Nissen hut, put a roof on the pig-sty, built up the walls of the pig-run and re-roofed it. We had made a compost heap and accumulated a very good assortment of tools and equipment. And during that first year when the only produce we had from the garden was the soft fruit, gifts of vegetables were so regular, plentiful and almost overwhelming that we had no cause to buy any at all, except perhaps mushrooms. We did briefly consider growing these but decided that we had more than enough to cope with. From then on we could look forward to a full cropping season and to being virtually self-sufficient.

CHAPTER SIX

In the days I am speaking of there was another route onto the allotment field which we sometimes took. This road wound through a fairly new small estate of bungalows and houses for a few hundred yards before becoming the cycle track - the converted railway line I have already mentioned.

In one of the bungalows along our route dwelt a very elderly childless couple, Edie and Edwin, who lived quietly and kept to themselves - that is, except for Edie's forays here and there to visit friends in the village for tea, and sometimes much further afield across the city. Our own elderly neighbour who regularly invited Edie to tea, and was entertained in return, used to say that she, Edie, would "rather walk two miles than spend fifty pence on bus fares". One wondered whether this rather spiteful observation may well have been true when, on returning one afternoon from a visit to friends on the other side of the city, and having walked home, Edie collapsed as she entered the bungalow and fell dead in the doorway between the kitchen and the dining room.

Edwin, who had been at home waiting for her to make his tea, found this abrupt turn of events very inconvenient. Neighbours were summoned and an ambulance called for, but on being told that the lady was already dead the ambulance declined to come, suggesting instead - in the circumstances - that the undertaker was the correct person to contact. There was a great deal of running about the house by several neighbours. Their priority was to contact the doctor and the undertaker by telephone but all the time Edwin was wanting his tea. In the course of attending to these contradictory requirements every journey made from kitchen to dining room and back again, either to the telephone or to set the tea-table, necessitated stepping over the corpse that lay in the intervening doorway. Eventually however Edwin was provided with a good tea - ham, salad, bread and butter, and plenty of strong, sweet tea - and the doctor had visited and certified the decease. At length, thereafter, the body of little Edie was removed by the undertaker, the neighbours went home, and Edwin settled down with his evening paper.

Back to the allotment route I was describing. Having passed the last house on the little estate, and reached the cycle track, there was an entrance to an Organic Nursery which at that time was a somewhat half-hearted project. (It would though, in a few years' time, have its fortunes revitalised consequent upon it obtaining funds from the National Lottery.) Then past open fields and what had been Black Bob's orchard and down a shady little path to a stile. Once through the stile it was 'turn right' to the Council estate or 'turn left' along a very narrow path.

This path, partly overgrown with grass, nettles and brambles to scratch your legs if you were not well covered, led to the entrance to the allotment field from the end opposite to that gained from the road and the gate. L. liked to take this route. It was traffic-free and wonderfully quiet, and on a warm summer's day with the birds singing and the insects humming, and the scent of the grass and of Iris's flowers and the mixed smells of vegetables in varying stages of growth and decay, one could be fifty miles from the nearest habitation. (And who, you will wonder, was Iris? Iris was a member of the Royal Horticultural Society and had a wonderful collection of unusual flowers on her allotment. She cycled to it from a nearby village and sometimes spent the whole day there, cooking pans of vegetables for her lunch.)

Arriving at the garden we leaned our bicycles against the sheds and sat on the seat for a while, our bodies absorbing the warmth and our minds relaxing in the comparative quietness and the knowledge that we had 'escaped'. The need to escape is in most of us at some time or another. For some escaping means flying off to the hot sun and a sandy beach or to climb high, lonely peaks, but for us a five-minute cycle ride to the gardens was enough to put the required space between us and the door and telephone bells and other calls on our attention.

CHAPTER SEVEN

The allotment field viewed from the bridge above it presented a sight very much like hundreds of other allotment fields, much less tidy and less organised than some but nevertheless more ground given over to cultivation than on a great many sites.

Its heterogeneous collection of huts and sheds were to many people an eyesore, but to others they had become Allotment Art. Some ingenuity went into the construction of these sheds. One or two were purpose-built and divided into four units so that four plot-holders sharing one shed each had a quarter, and each a separate entrance. We never knew of four people sharing one shed, though in several cases one shed was shared by two people.

Our own sheds, as already described, had in a former existence been a War-time Nissen hut and a pig-sty and pig-run, but others' sheds had been constructed from whatever materials were available and cheap: odd planks of wood, odd doors from demolition sites, bed frames and old enamel signs, with windows bodged up from old pieces of glass and with roofs of felt or canvas, tarred and made weatherproof. One resembled a covered wagon, another looked like a tent. Matt had two plots and two sheds, one of which accommodated a very large and comfortable armchair, given to him by a young affluent plotholder who was replacing furniture in his sitting-room. "It's a better chair than those I have at home", said Matt.

I have already described how L. restored the Nissen hut, and the other shed, half of which had been a pig-sty and half the pig-run. The door opened into the pig-run, now more agreeably re-named the Summer House. Across the back of it L. had made a long, wide seat covered with a layer of plastic foam which could be used as a bed, if anyone felt the urge to spend a night on it instead of being on a comfortable bed at home. L. kept threatening to come and sleep on this make-shift bed, and then in the morning to light a fire, boil water for tea in an ancient kettle saved from some house removal, and to fry bacon and sausages for breakfast.

But the plan never came to fruition; the comfort of his own bed after a day's toil with spade and fork being too much of an attraction, even for an old Boy Scout.

He had also constructed a single drop-leaf table with a formica top, put together from items of marine ply from the nearby boatyard where he happened to keep a small boat (in truth the boat rarely made contact with the water and was really for no more than dry-land sailing). L's general ingenuity knew no bounds. The front of the Summer House looked innocent enough from the outside, but inside, by a devious system of strings and hinges, an opening could be effected and a shelf dropped down from which we had planned to serve tea to our friends and neighbours. In fact this fanciful situation never came about because we were always far too busy.

When we took over these sheds there were several nesting boxes in the pig-run/Summer House, and we later learned that the year prior to our occupation Ernest had fattened up a turkey there. A long concrete trough from the pig era ran the length of the hut and I soon had designs on this for summer bedding plants at home, but it was firmly cemented in position - pigs being well known for uprooting almost everything - so there it had to stay.

We hung our strings of onions here in the Summer House but could not leave any other crops about; little animals, mice or voles perhaps, or even rats would soon have gobbled them up. Bees of a species unknown to us had a nest somewhere in the dark recesses of these buildings in the summer months. They were like small bumble bees, 'Day Bees' Matt called them. They wove their way in and out through a gap at the bottom of the door. We made sure we did not disturb them, and they in turn left us alone.

Early in our occupation it became evident why L. had been so interested in the sheds. He was looking for somewhere to store two or three (or more) bicycles. It was at a time when he was collecting vintage machines. We belonged to a Bygone Bikes club and from time to time we were offered suitable examples by people who realised that they were collectors' items. Three of them came from a nearby clergyman and one - a carrier bike - from the village butcher. The garage at home could not accommodate any more bicycles, so the pig-sty became the cycle store. And not only that, it housed the rotovator and the new wheelbarrow which we never used, preferring instead the old broken-down ones from Black Bob's orchard. In the new barrow and in the galvanised bath and enamel bowls we stored lime and 'Growmore'. It was not necessary to unlock, unbolt and open the door into the Summer House every time we turned up to work on the garden - the Black House held our immediate necessities, and at the end of the cropping season it became so congested that we could hardly step inside it.

One of the jobs for winter days was therefore 'a bit of shed work', when we would gather together into a plastic sack all the marker-sticks ready to be painted again with white emulsion before the Spring; roll up the lines tidily and sort out those decorated with shiny bits of metallic 'paper' or plastic to frighten the birds; put together into a carton the plastic bottles we had up-ended on bamboo poles amongst the peas and which rattled in the wind, *ditto* the bird-scarers; gather up old bits of wood and anything else burnable ready for the next bonfire; sort out the glove box usually holding at least six or seven pairs and always more for the left hand than for the right (and all in varying stages of dis-repair), and investigate the bottles, tins and packets to see what needed renewing and replacing when next we visited Mr Skilbeck's cavernous shop - of which more in the next chapter.

During the winter these occasions spent poking about in the sheds always proved more interesting than we expect-ed. Small items which had been 'mislaid' for weeks or even months turned up on the floor behind a sack of wood or a plastic carrier of string: a favourite pair of scissors, or a knife, a small trowel and even my 'best' secateurs. I 'lost' so may small tools about in the garden that L. eventually bound the handles with bright red or yellow tape so that they could easily be seen.

The sheds were tidy again and we could walk from one end to the other. For how long? For the present, anyhow.

CHAPTER EIGHT

About a mile down the road towards the city was another group of allotments. Each garden here was half the size of those on our site, in fact they were the normal size, ours at six-hundred-and-sixty square yards were double plots. This group of plots was affiliated to the Allotment Association and ran a shop, of sorts. We decided that we ought to become members of the Association and duly presented ourselves one Sunday morning to be enrolled. Forty pence each per annum. The shop opened twice a week, Sunday mornings from about 10.30 to 12 noon and Wednesday afternoons 2.30 to 4pm, times being approximate.

The shop building was an old railway goods van. The doorway was so low that anyone over five-foot-four-inches tall had to stoop to be able to enter without receiving a crack on the skull. The interior, being windowless, was rather dark and cave-like, the only light coming from the low and open doorway. The interior floor was filled so full with sacks and bags that there was very little room for more than two people to manoeuvre in and out and go up to the ancient desk, where sat Mr Claude Skilbeck at the receipt of custom.

A tall, bony man with a shock of grizzled white hair and enormous feet, he was bent with age and arthritis and possibly with years of negotiating the low doorway. It was said by the few people left who had known him in his youth - for he was now well over eighty - that he was of African origin (and had thus acquired the nickname of 'Darkie') and that he had shown great prowess with the cricket bat for his club as a young man. L. remembers on summer evenings in the early 1930s - when the local cricket clubs were playing matches - that he and his young teenage friends would hear the cry, "Darkie Skilbeck is batting" and would rush to the nearby cricket pitch to see him in action. Darkie was a 'big hitter' and therefore it was both attractive and exciting to watch his stroke play and see the ball being hit all over the ground. Thirty years later our own son as a young boy was similarly entranced to see this by now veteran batsman, nearing sixty years of age, still able to score runs for his team. And here he was in his old age, presiding over the allotment shop.

Under his watchful eye we could buy 'Growmore', slug pellets, potting and seed compost, and a variety of pest- and weed-killers and so forth. And in very early Spring, as we were either driving or cycling past, we looked for the words POTATOES and ONION SETS chalked on the end of the hut announcing that indeed the seed potatoes and the onion sets had arrived.

We mostly served ourselves to save Mr S. struggling onto his old feet and shuffling over to the sacks which were positioned around the massive weighing scales. And as we did so he shouted warnings to us from the desk not to drop the 'Stone' and 'Half-Stone' weights onto our feet. And we reached down from the shelves Jeyes fluid, decanted into wine and spirit bottles and roughly labelled 'Jeys' (sic) over the top of more delectably labelled contents, 'Navy' Rum, 'Martell' Brandy and the like. And the prices were, of course, correspondingly lower than those charged in the shops in town and in the garden centres.

Nearer still to the city was yet another group of allotments with a much larger shop housed in a proper purpose-built shed with windows, and set out in ship-shape fashion with racks of seed packets hanging on the walls, sacks of everything you could think of in orderly ranks on the floor, and all the smaller items neatly stacked on the shelves. Presiding over this emporium behind a long and wide counter were two or three old men, and another man about fifty in rolled-up shirt sleeves marching about in a business-like manner and obviously in charge. The old men behind the counter, who were eagerly waiting to pounce on customers should they make any sign of making a purchase or requiring assistance, looked as though they had been born and bred in the earth of an allotment. They were attired rather like garden gnomes, and their burned and wrinkled faces resembled very old potatoes.

On one of our visits here, in unseasonably cold weather with a temperature barely above freezing, one of these ancient brown men remarked to me, "It's sharp out there". "Yes," I replied, "and there's worse to come" - having recently heard the weather forecast. At this the little man almost exploded and said loudly, "I'm sick o' folks telling me how bad t'weather's goin' to be," and then suddenly fell silent as though surprised and alarmed by his own outburst. So I said diplomatically, "Well, we'll have to wait and see," and having returned to his normal taciturn manner he nodded agreement.

These two groups of allotments were unfortunately subject to a lot of thieving of crops. This was possibly because they were nearer to the city and close to busy roads. We were lucky, the only time we experienced the theft of vegetables was once or twice a year when there was a popular Race meeting, the racecourse being fairly near at hand and the thieves being gipsies, here for the racing and camped not far away. Potatoes, carrots and onions were the most popular as they could be dug up quickly. Thieves dared not stop long enough to pick peas, beans or soft fruit.

Members of the animal kingdom helped themselves fairly regularly, and birds especially were a real nuisance. One or two plotholders much younger than ourselves had built fruit cages to protect their raspberries and redcurrants, and they appeared to be very successful, in fact we felt sure that the birds, frustrated by not being able to get at the fruit in the cages, all flocked to our fruit bushes and gorged themselves into a drunken stupor on our redcurrants (our friend Tom swears he has seen blackbirds hardly able to walk or fly after a feeding session). All this in spite of our attempts to keep the birds off with green netting thrown over the bushes and a pretend hawk made by L. from a big parsnip for the body, a potato for the head and several long feathers for the tail and wings, fastened onto a long bendy stick which moved about in the wind. As the fruit ripened it became a contest as to who would get the berries first, the birds or me. So we devised a rather complicated and awkward method of securing the nets over the cluster of redcurrant bushes. This entailed L. climbing up a pair of steps and crawling onto the roof of the Summer House to trap the net onto the roof with bricks; then draping the netting over and around the bushes and tying it at the corners just above ground level.

It soon became obvious that the only way to harvest the fruit was to wait until it was all ripe and then early in the morning to remove the nets and spend the rest of the day picking and dealing with the fruit. This proved to be a very satisfactory method, and thus each year in early July the first suitably fine day was proclaimed Red Currant Day.

We would arrive at the plot at about half-past eight in the morning. This was comparatively early for us but we were well aware that some plotholders often started their gardening day at five o'clock or even earlier. We brought several large containers, a packed lunch and plenty of drinks - hot and cold - and sun hats if needed. It was really a very pleasant task, sometimes sitting on a stool, sometimes kneeling on a mat, picking the strings - like necklaces - of these luscious red berries and quickly filling a small bucket with them, though I have to say that after almost a whole day's work it did become rather wearisome. It made me think that I would not care to earn my living picking redcurrants; and no wonder they were so expensive in the supermarkets. Picking the fruit was not the end of it - those which we did not give away had to be cleaned and then either cooked, jellied or frozen.

On one of these Red Currant Days, as we were taking off the nets, I found a dead sparrow which had become entangled in the netting and which had actually decapitated itself in its struggles to get free. This was quite upsetting and I put it to one side intending to give it a decent burial. As we began picking, a very nice friendly cat which lived nearby wandered over to us and rubbed itself against our legs. Its owners were away and it wanted company, so we thought, and we made a fuss of it. Then it spied the sparrow's corpse and quickly snatched it up and made off with it. This was, I suppose, preferable to seeing the cat catch and run off with a live bird.

CHAPTER EIGHT

And so Red Currant Day came to a close for another year. The nets were shaken clear of leaves and twigs, rolled up and stored away in the summer house. And then there was the rather tedious task of stringing the currants and packing them into the freezer. But what a treat it was on a dull, cold January day to bring out a box of redcurrants, gently cook and sweeten them, and make a deep, ruby-red tart. A taste of summer in the depth of winter.

CHAPTER NINE

There was a resident pheasant in the orchard just waiting for us all to sow our beans. Broad beans, Runner beans or French beans, all were equally attractive to it and what is more it knew exactly where they were, digging them up very neatly leaving the exit holes in the earth and other trade marks. We spent a great deal of time and effort weaving long lengths of black cotton from one end of the row to the other, fastened to nails which were hammered into pieces of wood resembling table-tennis bats, but to no avail. This bird got wise to all our tricks and indeed had a few of its own. The only way to stop the thieving was to grow the beans in pots at home and plant them out when they were about six inches tall.

Matt wanted L. to shoot the pheasant, and he would have done so had I not protested; Matt had worked on farms and was not so soft-hearted about killing pests as I was. He had at one time kept hens on the allotments and spent £8 a week on hen food which he said was all eaten by rats and starlings, in fact "I fed all the rats and starlings in the village," he said. So he set up his own rat-trap. This was a cage with a door which was held up by a stick attached to a rope at one edge. Matt and a friend sat in his shed sharing a bottle of beer and waiting for the rats to come, and when they were all feeding on the bait in the cage he pulled the rope and the rats were trapped. Matt then killed them with an airgun and caught seventeen rats in this manner, "But," he said, "it was a slow business". He teased me - at least I hope it was teasing - by saying that he had put dead rats in the bottom of the Runner bean trench.

Cats from nearby homes wandered around the gardens and would sit about in the long grass perhaps looking for mice or birds, but we found them to be friendly on the whole and rather lazy and aloof. They did have an irritating habit of deliberately walking on a finely raked bed of earth ready for sowing, leaving their distinct paw-marks in the soil. And some plot-holders brought their dogs with them when they came to work on their plots, but these animals were always kept well under control. Compared to some allotment sites we were quiet and untroubled, with little thieving from either humans or animals.

* * *

We had often wondered what it was like after nightfall down on the gardens, and so on one June night, on the eve of the Summer Solstice, we decided to go and find out.

It was fine and still just before midnight as we cycled slowly to the gate, opening and closing it as quietly as possible. No sounds, but one or two lights in the houses and the occasional car driving home late. We leaned our bicycles against the Black House and sat on the seat looking at the Western sky. Even at midnight it was not completely dark - there was still a faint after-glow through the thin clouds. Gradually the house lights were extinguished and we were wrapped around by the soft semi-darkness. A moth fluttered around us and we wondered what other creatures of the night, under the ground or above it in the grass and hedges, were busy with their nocturnal lives. The burgeoning vegetation smelled fresh and clean in the night air, waiting for the coming day to soak up the moisture and the sunlight and put forth more growth. A slight breeze ruffled the trees and we imagined the birds asleep in their nests and roosting in the branches for a few short hours, for this was the shortest night of the year. Soon with the dawn they would wake and begin their never-ending search for food, and people and machines too would start their relentless noisy, daily toil. But for just a while there was a wonderful silence. The Earth around us was sleeping. And we too crept quietly home to rest.

CHAPTER TEN

By the time we had been working the plot for about five years we were pretty well organised. We cultivated the whole double-plot area, practising crop rotation religiously and rigorously, and drew plans with colour-coding (ROOTS, BRASSICAS, OTHERS) to see that we did it properly. We had our problems of course. Club root, aforementioned, was one to which we never found a solution, another was the carrot fly. We certainly had not the time or the energy to erect barriers to stop this pest in its flight. But we were harvesting good crops each season, though as all allotment gardeners know not all crops are successful every year. My cupboards at home resembled Badger's store of food ('Badger' from *The Wind in the Willows*) with their shelves full of jam (blackcurrant and raspberry), pickled onions and chutneys. A large freezer had been bought after the first season of soft fruit and now it was packed with rhubarb, red currants, rasps, gooseberries, black currants and blackberries. Then there were the vegetables to freeze, and Oh, all that blanching in the freezing process. But they kept us self-sufficient all year round, interspersed in the winter with our own fresh root vegetables and with Matt's Brussels sprouts and cabbages. We were just finishing one year's frozen produce as the new season's fruit was ripening on the bushes.

A kind of bartering system had evolved between plotholders, and to facilitate the exchange of goods which were available L. had made a small notice board and fastened it to the outside wall of the pig-run near to one of the troughs and easily readable from the green path. On it one could advertise - for example - cabbage plants, or leek seedlings, or - say - two or three courgette plants and any surplus seeds. The plants and seeds on offer were always free and thus everyone benefited. Sometimes an item of machinery was offered for sale, and this saved the vendor the expense of advertising in the local paper. L. found himself asked to repair one or two sheds and received as payment vegetables which we did not grow ourselves -

tomatoes, cucumbers and gherkins, and more exotic items such as aubergines and peppers.

We were sure that our health was better due to the exercise and all the hours spent in the open air, and we were, in a way, sailing along quite comfortably when L. got this itch to take on part of another plot which had been vacant for some time and had therefore become neglected. It must have been the shed again which attracted him, and having negotiated with the Parish Clerk, and put new locks on the shed door, it was ours, or rather it was his because I was less than enthusiastic about it. We christened this newly acquired shed The Temple, and as well as finding a Grecian-style Victorian kitchen chair inside it, with sundry tins and bottles of plant food and pest killer, we discovered that a very nice cat sometimes came in through a space under the door and slept on a pile of rags which we left there for it.

Then there were the strawberries, and I could not resist those, and spent a lot of time digging out the couch grass from amongst them and covering the rows of plants with big wire frames acquired from a nearby villager. We had a reasonably good crop of strawberries and L. planted potatoes ('to help clear the ground') and cabbages and cauliflowers - as this plot seemed to be free from club root - and we had quite good results.

But after a couple of seasons L. had to admit that it was all too much and we were glad to hand it over to our new young neighbour at home who was looking for a plot, though I was aware that L. - being unwilling to relinquish completely the tenancy of the shed - still kept a key to The Temple and housed a few surplus items there - just to retain a presence so to speak.

We were getting older. L. was now well over seventy and I was on the way to it, and our six-hundred-and-sixty square yards was beginning to feel like a couple of acres. We discussed ways and means of cutting down on the work and the area we were cultivating without actually surrendering any of the land. Perhaps rather selfishly we wanted to keep the whole plot to ourselves and not have another plotholder working half of it and maybe putting up a shed on it. It was a conflicting situation to be in. On the one hand cultivating the whole plot was proving to be too much for us, but on the other hand we did not want to part with it to anyone else. Dog in the manger? Almost a classic case of it. But there seemed to be no urgency to come to any decision.

This was one of the many pleasures we found in allotment gardening. The lack of urgency automatically brought relaxation. What was not done today would get done tomorrow, or in a few days' time. What did it matter if we were a week or two late in sowing broad beans? - they would soon catch up when they eventually germinated. And so we jogged along as yet unaware that in the near future changes were on the way which would turn all our gardening lives upside down and, for better or worse, make some of the decisions for us.

CHAPTER ELEVEN

The allotment field was owned by the Church Commissioners and rented out to the Local Authority. This was no new development or arrangement. There had been allotments on the site for over a hundred years, but the history of allotment gardening went back much further than that. Four hundred years ago peasants had been 'allotted' a piece of land to grow food to help to feed their families after the enclosure of common lands. Then, as the movement of people from the country to the town began in the nineteenth century, allotments appeared in towns as well, usually instigated by local philanthropists to help to alleviate poverty. By the first Allotment Act of 1887, and the later Act of 1922, "all local authorities are under a statutory obligation to provide allotment gardens for all suitable persons provided application is made by six registered electors or six ratepayers residing in the district".

During the property boom of the late 1980s the Church Commissioners had been financially ill-advised and had invested heavily in property. After the market plunged in 1990 the scale of the loss that ensued was immense and they had no less than eight-hundred million pounds wiped off their assets. In the light of this loss and with an eye to recouping it (even though the Church of England's total assets were over two billion pounds), they took to selling off farmland, residential holdings and city-centre shops which were in their ownership. Suddenly our little allotment field of only 3.3 acres became very valuable to them and another source of capital if sold to one of the local building firms.

Rumours of what was in the wind soon spread among the plotholders and caused great consternation. The District Planning Officer was consulted - and yes, plans had been drawn up for residential building on the whole field. In other words without informing anyone at our level of their intentions, the Church Commissioners had decided to offer the land for building, and a building firm had drawn up plans and presented them to the Local Authority.

SCENES FROM AN ALLOTMENT GARDEN

What were we to do? Here on this very site was a way of life which had been quietly rolling along for over a hundred years. In those early days of the nineteenth century men had cultivated the soil out of necessity, using rough tools and with none of the conveniences and amenities which we largely take for granted; and as social and economic conditions improved over the years - and the need to grow food was not quite so desperate - whole families had enjoyed being able to work on their plots in the open air, often after a long day's toil in a noisy mill or a stifling office. People who could never have afforded a holiday derived an enormous amount of pleasure and satisfaction from the time spent out of doors, sowing their seeds and harvesting their vegetables, fruit and flowers.

Was this village tradition to be lost for yet another housing estate to provide more money for a building firm? And to help bail the Church of England out of financial difficulties for which its Commissioners were responsible? Some of our number, blissfully unaware of the machinations of those in charge of the Church finances, were appalled to realise that we could be turned off our land by the Church, of whom, until now, they had had such a high opinion. But as realisation of what was going on sunk in, they reared up and declared that they would cease to put their weekly offering into the collecting bag at the Sunday service as it would be needed more urgently to buy vegetables and fruit if they were no longer able to grow them.

Some of us knew that an allotment site could not be disposed of unless an alternative site was offered. This alternative had to be "equal in size to the old one, meet the local demand, be suitable for spade cultivation and be within reasonable distance of people's homes", to quote the Allotment Act 1925, restated in the Town and Country Planning Act 1959.

We speculated on what possible alternative site could be offered to meet these demands, but first we needed support to campaign against the planning proposals. So who were we to approach? First the Parish Council and then the Local Authority. Letters were written to both, objecting in strong terms to any building plans. The actual plans which had been submitted (for forty-one houses) were obtained from the local planning office and we studied these with growing concern. We received acknowledgement of our letters but no definite word of support. This was hardly surprising as we knew that for every new house built the Local Authority received money from the government - at that time - and not only that, there would be the Council Tax from forty-one new houses to swell their coffers. People who lived near to the Allotment field on the road leading to the gate were keen to lend us their support. This gate was proposed by the building firm as being the new and only access to the planned building site. The residents on this road certainly did not want dozens of cars turning in and out of a new roadway almost on their doorsteps.

We next approached the man who we felt had more influence than anyone else - at least as far as the Church Commissioners were concerned - the Archbishop of York himself. By this time we had learned that two alternatives to our present allotment site had been proposed. It was obvious to us all that both were entirely unsuitable for allotment gardening and did not meet the standards demanded by the law already cited, i.e. "meet local demand, be within reasonable distance, and be suitable for spade cultivation". His Grace was fairly non-commital but promised to pass on our letters to the Commissioners.

All these negotiations were long and protracted and took place during the height of the cropping season. And so we all carried on, hoeing our plots, picking the fruit, the peas and the beans, and cutting the courgettes and lettuces, but with a shadow over all our activities. None of us knew what was going to happen next, or when, but no one was very optimistic. From time to time we would take a break from our gardening tasks and sit on a seat, or stand in a group speculating on what the next move would be, where it would come from and which of us would be most affected.

Then towards the end of the year an On-Site meeting was called, by the Local Authority, between the Planning Committee and the plotholders and their supporters. The plotholders turned out in force and the meeting was held just within the gate off the public highway.

Those of us who had hoped to speak and put forward our views were soon silenced by the officious chairman of the Committee who would allow only one spokesman from our ranks. Fortunately, while our nominated speaker was pointing out the dangers of access into and out of the site, there was such a volume of traffic on the road that the Committee had no hesitation in refusing planning permission.

We breathed a collective sigh of relief, but we were not complacent. We knew only too well that a new application would be made, suggesting an alternative place of access to the site. And indeed it was.

After a further appeal to the Archbishop, in which I pointed out that we would lose the last tranquil open space in the village should the allotment field be sold for residential building, he decreed, in a gesture reminiscent of the judgement of Solomon, that half the field should be built on and the other half kept as allotments.

This was, I suppose, more than we had hoped for. In my worst moments I had visualised the whole field desecrated and filled with houses. I was well aware that a section of the community would have liked this to happen: "Get rid of those awful sheds"..., "Let us have more smart new houses with tidy gardens", and, "I like to buy nice clean vegetables at the supermarket", were some of the comments I listened to. Even one of the local Councillors wanted more houses for families which would bring more children to swell the numbers at the village schools and therefore attract more Government funding to them. But we had, through our efforts and our campaigning, saved half the field from the developers. We would keep some allotments and those who wanted new houses would have them.

Meanwhile meetings were held between the plotholders and the Church Commissioners' representatives, and the dividing line between retained allotment and new building land was worked out. It became clear as a result of this that the line that had been drawn would cut three metres,

lengthways, off our own plot, which happened to be nearest to the building line. This was not totally unexpected; we
knew that our plot was very near to the half-way mark.
However it did seem a bit pernickety to divide the field
exactly in half to the very last inch (or centimetre); we felt
that a dividing line which did not cut into anyone's plot
would have been more sympathetic. But it seemed Shylock
must have his pound of flesh: those with plots on the building-land half of the garden moved to vacant plots on the
allotment half, and things settled down again, albeit somewhat uneasily.

*   *   *

And so it had become a reality. From the first whisper-
ings of residential development and our initial anxieties,
through the enquiries, the meetings, the protests and the
campaigning, here were the facts in front of us. Half the
field would be lost to new housing, half would be retained
as allotments. The Church Commissioners would benefit
financially; so would the building firm. The allotment gardeners were the losers whichever way one cared to look at
it as I will relate in due course. Our quiet, friendly allotment
field would never be the same again.

CHAPTER TWELVE

We took to walking up and down the three-metre strip which we would lose - looking across the open land, which though it had become a wilderness was nevertheless a tranquil open space as yet undefiled by new buildings - and we tried not to visualise the eventual outcome. But with the impending loss of land and the imminent building work also came the realisation that we no longer felt able to cultivate our six-hundred-and-sixty square yards of allotment garden. This had been in our minds for some time as I have already said, but the changes on the land which were about to take place had taken precedence over any plans we might have had to alter our own workload. But now we had to do something.

The thought of reducing our scope was not entirely gloomy and depressing. 'Set-Aside' for farmers had become fashionable just at this time, so why not a bit of 'set-aside' for us? We therefore gave up the cultivation of one third of what we called 'The Field' and it rapidly reverted to grass. On this section was a greengage tree which we had brought from the garden at home several years earlier. It had hardly ever produced a plum, partly due to late frosts catching the blossom and partly due to the fact that there was no suitable pollinator near at hand even though Black Bob's orchard was just over the hedge. So we now moved a Victoria plum from home to keep it company and in the hope that one would pollinate the other. We moved this tree on a trailer attached to the car, to the turning-round area on the allotments just beyond our sheds and then on one of Black Bob's rusty old wheelbarrows to its new home. One of the plotholders who was moving from the building-land half gave us a Golden Delicious tree and together with a Grenadier (also from home) in no time at all we had the beginnings of an orchard. Matt gave us two silver birch saplings and the following Spring we had clumps of bluebells and solidago growing wild. I filled several old containers with soil and compost and sowed wild flower seeds in them and it all became quite delightful. We regularly mowed the grass, and here we would sit on two rickety chairs up to a makeshift table with a flask of tea and pieces of fruit cake and sometimes a picnic lunch, almost hidden from view by the broad bean plants and the bramble hedge.

We half buried an old dustbin lid in the grass and filled it with water for the birds and found that it soon attracted a little hedgehog. We discovered more wildlife in one of the compost bins. Lifting up the cover one day we were surprised to see two or three very fat mice which scuttled out of sight deep into the morass of vegetable waste and soil. We liked to take the mice unawares by tiptoe-ing to the bin then quickly lifting the cover and watching them running hither and thither until they burrowed out of sight. It must have been like a five-star mouse hotel for them. Perhaps during the winter the hedgehog lived there as well; there were holes and tunnels in one of the bins so it seemed quite likely. We therefore left the compost undisturbed all winter.

Thus we all carried on with our allotment gardening, not exactly as though nothing had happened, more in a sort of limbo, wondering where the next move would come from and when.

* * *

By now we had become experienced enough to know what crops we grew well and which were a waste of time and effort. Most brassicas came into this latter category and we had given up some years previously trying to grow cauliflowers and Brussels sprouts. But we were very successful in growing beans, using all our own seed, and we regularly harvested good crops of onions, potatoes and courgettes. We experimented with fancy and colourful varieties of lettuce, Red Salad Bowl, Lollo Rossi and Tiger with good results, and with garlic and Egyptian onions. But always in the back of our minds was the question, "when will the building work start?"

L's last creative effort on the garden was to build what I called 'The Arty Fence' the length of our plot next to the building line, "to show the builders our plot boundary". This fence was constructed entirely from material close at hand, and into it went a single-bed frame, a discarded gate (from one of our neighbours), the clothes horse which had belonged to Matt's mother, two wheels from a Mini, frames of garden chairs (the canvas seats and backs having perished) and other items of similar provenance. And along the fence we planted brambles which quickly took hold and entwined themselves around the artefacts. Perhaps in doing this we were deluding ourselves and pretending that what was to come would never happen and that in the Autumn we would be picking the brambles.

A vain pretence, because at last the time came - almost two years after the first negotiation began - when strange men were seen hammering thick, orange-coloured stakes into the ground four or five feet into the width of our plot and down the length of it. A few days later a mechanical digger appeared on what had now become wasteland waiting to be built on. We questioned the digger driver and were told that they had come to investigate what lay under the surface of the top soil, and they discovered it to be marl; so we went home and looked that up in our reference books.

It was fascinating to find that in the seventeenth and eighteenth centuries marl was used as a fertiliser, particularly in Lancashire and Cheshire, where it was found in large quantities. It was dug out of pits by gangs of men, but by the middle of the nineteenth century with the railways able to transport cheaper fertilisers, marling died out, although when discussing it with Matt he told me that there had been marl pits in our own area up to about 1930.

The end of the cropping season approached once more and with it came Harvest Festival. It had become our custom to transport in our estate car Matt's own considerable contribution to the Church harvest decorations. We thus arrived at his plot early on the Saturday morning the day before the Harvest Thanksgiving service. As usual he was ready for us, with a breath-taking array of freshly-washed carrots, swedes, leeks, beetroot, parsnips and potatoes, onions, runner beans, marrows of various sizes and colours and the showpiece of it all, one, or sometimes two gigantic orange-coloured pumpkins.

We displayed it all in the Church Baptistry, and for me this symbolised the true meaning of Harvest Thanksgiving. Though Harvest Festival is not an ancient institution in itself these offerings, together with rows of apples and pears in the windowsills of the nave and the traditional bread in the form of a wheatsheaf placed in the sanctuary, showed man's affinity with the earth and his continuing ability over the centuries to produce, by the labours of his hands, good wholesome food.

The end of this particular cropping season also brought at last the beginning of the dreaded building work, and devastation was soon to ensue.

CHAPTER THIRTEEN

The trees and the hedge which formed the southern boundary of the plots, and which were part of Black Bob's orchard, were chopped down together with the fruit trees in the orchard. Alas for the birds; they would have to find alternative accommodation. There would be no more apples for anyone to help themselves to and no more wind-falls for the birds to peck. Even though we knew what would happen, actually to see the destruction of a small wild-life area filled us with dismay and we watched with heavy hearts as the greed for yet more land and more money manifested itself.

The half of the allotment field which had been designated as building land had quickly become a wilderness and soon the diggers moved in and churned it up: all except the shed we had known as The Temple - that stood alone in the wasteland for some weeks waiting for specialists to demolish it and remove its asbestos roof. The great lumbering machines gobbled up the earth far more quickly than we had anticipated and there was now some urgency to save what crops we could as the diggers began to encroach on the three metres of land which we were losing.

The next in line for destruction was L's 'Arty Fence', and "showing the builders our plot boundary" was soon all swept away into the skip. We began to feel like trespassers on our own plot and we hurriedly dug up three gooseberry bushes and moved them to safer ground. One of our black-currant bushes and a redcurrant bush were chopped down and more than a dozen raspberry canes uprooted. We rushed to dig up leeks, parsnips and beetroot in the path of the machines, and we replanted the rasp canes in the orchard along with the gooseberry bushes, not too hopeful for their survival after such indignities.

One of the builder's labourers, when he was at a loose end, helped us to move our manure heap in barrow-loads to a new site and L. would titivate all our sheds with rust-coloured paint so that even to the builders it did not look too much like a gipsy encampment, and they may just show some respect for our presence there.

Meanwhile the main gate from the public highway was removed and replaced by steel barriers through which there was no access. The huge bulldozer dug a vast trench all along the green path from the gate to our sheds to bring the top-water drain to the building site. Sheds in its path were demolished, but those who lost their sheds could either have the old one moved to a new site or have a new shed built at the builder's expense. Matt had a ceremonial burning of his old brown shed when his new one was built.

The only access now from the gateway to the plots was through a snicket in the hedge. We then had to pick our way, carefully criss-crossing over several other plots to our own, which was furthest from the gateway. The green path had completely gone, dug to a depth of two metres to take the water pipes. There was almost incessant rain during those winter months and the two-metre trench was continually flooded in spite of pumping operations. Fred the pipeman and his team worked in appalling conditions and we really felt quite sorry for them in spite of what they were doing to our once green and tranquil gardens.

Our plot was now open on all sides to men and machines and we felt very vulnerable. We longed for the promised fence to be built across the bottom of the plot and up the east side of it. "The fencers are starting next week" was repeated to us time and time again by the site manager, week after week, and still we waited.

During those dark days and weeks we almost dreaded going to the garden. There was little we could do when we did go. Arriving at the barrier which had once been the gate we would look hopefully across the plots to see if the fencers had started work. But they had not done so, and all we could do was to take a depressing walk around the plot looking at the churned-up ground.

All through those winter months it seemed as though the devastation we had dreaded was complete.

CHAPTER FOURTEEN

The early days of Spring brought some hope of better things, not only an improvement in the weather and the longer hours of daylight but at last, after waiting seven weeks, work was started on the fence along the eastern boundary of our plot. It began by holes being dug to take concrete posts. This work had already been carried out along the southern boundary, and after another week the posts were put loosely into the holes. And there they remained, leaning at all angles like drunken men, for another two weeks. Finally at the end of February they were set upright in concrete.

During those weeks we had not been idle. We had spread manure where it was needed and cut dead wood out of the brambles and burned it. We still had a good supply of root vegetables to use and we took up Matt's offer to pick the last of the sprouts from his plot and to dig Sweet William plants for the garden at home. We enjoyed some pleasant late-February days when it was warm enough to take a flask of tea and a cake and to sit on the seat, with our backs to the development site and the uncompleted fence and looking instead at the more pleasing aspect across the plots which remained intact.

It was now time to buy seed potatoes and onion sets and new packets of vegetable seeds, having looked through the old shoe-box of last year's seed packets to see if any could still be used. L. thought it would be a good idea to grow potatoes at the southernmost extremity of the plot where the hedge had been, "to clear the ground", a phrase I had heard before when we took over The Temple. I was horrified at the suggestion as I had seen not only the nettles but what turned out to be buckets-full of broken glass and metal rubbish, which we cleared away when we eventually got to work on the area, preparing it for the potatoes.

I spread spades-full of ash from our many bonfires around the gooseberry bushes and in doing so saw that some of the raspberry canes near to the fencing posts had been set in the concrete. The supports and wires for the canes, so carefully fixed in position in the first days of our occupancy, had been uprooted and tossed around the area. This was quite upsetting and I dug up what canes I could before the feet of the joiners could trample them down when they finally arrived to make the fence. In all we reckoned that we had lost about forty raspberry canes.

The plot next to us had become vacant, the tenants having moved to Wales, and rather than see what vegetables remained on it going to waste we all helped ourselves to them as no one came forward to rent the plot. I dug up red Dead Nettle from amongst the weeds on the plot, and these together with some daffodil bulbs and honeysuckle cuttings from home I planted in the orchard.

In the middle of March the joiners arrived and work began in earnest to construct the new fence. The men worked quickly and efficiently and in a matter of two or three days the fence was completed. It was a solid wooden fence, six feet high, and immediately gave us privacy, and we noticed that it would shelter us from the south and east winds.

There was now a formidable amount of clearing up to do on our side of the new fence. The first task was to make a path next to it so that we could walk along that side of the plot. Here L. was able to collect up pieces of new wood of varying lengths discarded by the joiners. And we picked up dozens of new nails and screws which they had dropped and either not had the time or could not be bothered to pick up again. So this particular job was not without its perks. Also on the 'plus' side of this operation was the unearthing of a very good cultivator from under the blackcurrant bushes which I had lost about a year previously. It all helped to lift our spirits.

We planted forty-three shallot bulbs, garlic cloves and Egyptian onions, and as we toiled to bring some order to what was left of our own plot things were also happening at the other side of the allotment field, where the original gate had opened onto the public highway.

CHAPTER FIFTEEN

The two-metre trench all along what had been the green path was at last filled in, but we had strict instructions from the workmen not even to walk on it let alone put a bicycle on it, and we would "not be able to drive a car on it for six months". So L. and I were still picking our way across the other plots to reach our own, which made it very awkward for us when we had heavy items to carry.

By the end of March we were all becoming restive. The new gate leading from the road onto the allotment field had not been hung; the promised hard-standing for cars inside the gate had not materialised; the no-longer-green path had not been re-seeded, and a new water tap - near to our sheds where the old one had been cut off by the builders - had not been fitted. We all felt that we were getting a raw deal. For almost six months we had put up with this monumental upheaval across the plots. We had all lost our access and our path; some of us had lost sheds; many of us had lost crops, all for a project which had nothing to do with us and from which none of us would benefit in any way at all. The inconvenience it had caused us was too much to be tolerated without a complaint, now that we appeared to have been abandoned and all the building work was now concentrated on the new housing development.

So a volley of letters of complaint from the plotholders was fired off to the Parish Council and to the builders, and in a week or two 'bore fruit', so to speak. An On-Site meeting was called between plotholders, Parish Council and some of the top brass from the building firm. As soon as the date of the meeting was known L. and I canvassed all the other plotholders to get as good an attendance as possible, and most people turned out. This meeting really gave us a chance to air our grievances. There was no bossy chairman to order us about this time and we could make known just what inconveniences we had endured and how our gardening lives had been disrupted. Not that we expected to be understood. In the builders' eyes we were very small fry. Building and selling new houses was their priority and no doubt they thought that their offer of a paltry amount of financial compensation for the loss of crops and so forth would put everything right for us.

And during those weeks of waiting as well as harvesting the first of the forced rhubarb we planted one-hundred-and-twenty-seven onion sets, sowed parsnip seeds and dug the runner bean trench and put manure in it. And we tackled the southern-most plot and planted potatoes in it, using the easy method of digging a hole with a trowel, dropping in a lump of manure and then a potato. Some of these seed potataoes were an unknown variety saved from last year's crop. Some were Ratty, which were like Pink Fir Apple but white. We were particularly partial to Pink Fir Apples, their nobbly shapes made them impossible to scrape but the skins were thin and delicate and the flesh waxy, and so everything was edible.

While working here on what we now called the south plot we were near to the new fence on the other side of which one of the new houses was now being built. From time to time we would find whole tomatoes, chocolate wrappers and sandwiches of white sliced, plastic-type bread and thin supermarket ham thrown over the fence and which had come to rest on the plot. Rejects from the work-men's packed lunches we supposed. In our accustomed thrifty manner we composted the tomatoes and cut up the sandwiches for the birds. The burnable rubbish went onto the next bonfire.

We adjusted ourselves to our altered conditions, to the narrower plot, to the new fence, to the extra work. L. began to prepare the 'Merry Tiller' rotovator for sale. He was find-ing it too heavy to handle and had already bought a small-er model second-hand from another plotholder. We sowed broad beans, leeks, red lettuce and cabbage seeds and had planted two more rows of potatoes, properly, in the trench-es which Matt had prepared for us. In fact we were manag-ing very well and pleased with what we had done in the face of all the difficulties.

The new gate was hung and the new water-tap fixed and working. Thus at the end of April we had hopes of a good and successful cropping season, though we were aware that we were not as active as we had been even a year ago. But the fruit bushes were burgeoning, the seeds we had sown were germinating, there was blossom on the fruit trees and the weather was warming up and reasonably dry. The trials of the last six months began to recede even though the evidence of what was happening was all around us. It was almost a case of 'everything in the garden was lovely', when disaster struck. At the very end of April L. ruptured his Achilles tendon.

CHAPTER SIXTEEN

L. was now eighty years old, and though he had always been so very active this accident, and six weeks with his leg in plaster, set him back a very great deal. He was completely unable to work in the garden and so I was left to tackle it alone, and there were very definite limits as to how much I could do.

But help was near at hand. As I sowed seeds of carrots and spring onions and covered the cabbage seedlings with wire tunnels, Matt filled the water butts for me and cut the grass on the paths and in the orchard. I put chicken wire over the lettuces and sowed seeds of swede and beetroot and Matt gave me Nicotiana seedlings for the garden at home, and sweet pea seedlings to train up the runner bean supports.

At the end of the first week in May work began on the green path. I cycled down one morning and saw a man raking the soil on the path. As I approached he lit up a big cigar, and as he carried on raking, sometimes with the cigar in his mouth, sometimes between his fingers as he raked, I asked him what was happening. He told me that a strip of turf was to be laid at one side of the green path wide enough for us to walk on. Then the rest of the path was to be re-seeded. And later that day men came with rolls of turf and soon had a narrow strip laid all the way to our sheds. This was something which L. had to see, so I drove him to the gate and he was able to get out of the car and stand with his crutches, leaning on the gate and looking at this latest development.

The new turf path was a great step forward, we could walk on it, wheel a bicycle on it and before very long ride a bike on it. I had cycled down one day and was sitting on our seat with Matt. We were discussing some uncultivated areas on our plot which he was offering to rotovate. A man who was a stranger to us both turned up and said he was renting the next plot to ours which had been vacant for some months. He told us how he would remove the dilapidated shed on the plot and build a new one, as well as all the other improvements he would make. When I returned home and reported this conversation to L. he was seriously alarmed. The reason for this was because he had fastened the main support of the runner bean row, a heavy iron bar, to the top of the dilapidated shed. And whatever would happen if the new plotholder came along within the next few days to demolish the shed? Would the iron bar come crashing down, possibly on his head, and with it the wooden stakes and bamboo poles which were permanently there to support the runner beans? Absolutely nothing could be done about it while L. was incapacitated. Each day I went to the garden in some trepidation to see what was happening. Would I find the shed flattened and the body of the new plotholder sticking out from under it? But as the days passed and no changes had taken place, gradually the anxiety of what might happen receded as the new tenant did not appear again and we heard that after all he was not renting the plot. Something had put him off. We wondered what it could have been.

It was now the middle of May and time to sow courgettes and sweetcorn in pots at home. Most of us had problems with courgette seeds. The germination rate was poor and it was no good returning the packet of seeds - or what was left in the packet - to the seed merchant with a covering letter of complaint. By the time they had replied and sent us a free packet of seeds (no better than the original ones) it was too late to sow them. We all knew this; we had tried it in previous years. We therefore sowed twice as many seeds as we needed in pots and hoped that, say, six out of twelve would germinate.

Having had his leg in plaster for almost three weeks and become very adept with his crutches, L. thought he would like to try hobbling down from the gate to the seat outside our sheds. So we drove to the gate and he managed very slowly to propel himself along the turf path. Having got to the seat and rested he then had a look at the plot and issued a few instructions on the preparation for sowing the French and Runner beans which was imminent.

This was now the busiest time of the season for us. Matt had transplanted my cabbage seedlings and done a lot of hoeing for me, and the next big task was to cover the fruit bushes with netting. He and I draped our green nets over and around the redcurrants, but covering the blackcurrants was a two-man job, and I was not tall enough to do it even with help. So Ted, who had a plot near to the gate, came to the rescue. Ted was a tall, spare, elderly man who often came to swop 'War in the Western Desert' experiences with L. as they sat on the seat for a breather. He used to say that he came to garden to get out from under his wife's feet, but he was a good gardener and produced excellent fruit and vegetables as well as an interesting line in scarecrows. So he and Matt took our big black nets and completely covered the row of blackcurrant bushes, all eleven yards of it. I handed out clothes pegs for them to clip the edges of the nets together. Thus all the difficult tasks were completed and as long as I hoed, weeded and watered, we could manage. I picked raspberries, redcurrants and gooseberries and froze what I did not immediately use or give away.

L. finally got out of plaster and though still not very mobile was able to ride his bicycle and then to drive the car. This I felt was really a step forward, and things were looking up. However within three weeks he was called into hospital for two operations which had been pending for some time and which were related to physical discomforts that had gradually made their presence felt during the preceding decade.

L. was no stranger to the operating theatre, so in the light of previous experiences perhaps we should have been prepared for the statement from the surgeon that his condition was serious. As it was, this news came as a great shock to us; instead of expecting him to return to the gardening scene fit and well in two or three weeks' time we realised that now we would have to come to terms with this being the beginning of the end of allotment gardening for us.

CHAPTER SEVENTEEN

The green path was green again and we were able to drive a car on it by the middle of August. There was some apprehension attached to this operation. We were the first to risk a vehicle on the new path; would we sink up to the axles and need a tractor to haul us out? Some of us watched anxiously as L. carefully trundled along from the gate to our plot. All was well. The path seemed solid and firm.

The allotment field had now taken on a new and unlovely look. How different it was from our first sight of the gardens twelve years ago. Then there was the quiet three-acre expanse of land. It was almost a little private enclave; the houses were far enough away in the distance not to overlook the gardens; there was the high hedge along the southern boundary, and Black Bob's orchard on the other side of it; the only sounds were of the birds, and in the summer the occasional rattling of the bird-scarers in the breeze; there always seemed to be plenty of room for us all to spread ourselves and our equipment around the plots, and there was space to stroll about and look at our neighbours' crops to see whether they were coming on better than ours.

Now towering above and all around us were the new detached houses, like great pink-and-yellow boxes full of eyes peering down onto the gardens and, we felt, onto our plot in particular. There was no longer the privacy we had known: the quietness seemed to have gone; the sense of space had gone; we all seemed to be crowded together and shut in by the new houses.

And later in the year as the days shortened and winter approached we realised that the sun never reached the bottom of our garden; the new houses shut it out completely. Certainly in summer when the sun was high it would shine on all the plot, but never again would the whole garden be bathed in sunshine during Autumn and Winter. Even if we had been able to carry on gardening we had doubts as to whether we would have wanted to retain this particular plot in these conditions, being constantly overlooked from only a few yards' distance and shaded from the sunshine. L. was now sufficiently recovered from his operations to be able to do some light work. He was able to cut the grass on the paths and in the orchard, and in this early Autumn we were harvesting good crops of beans, courgettes and potatoes and enjoying the fresh taste of the new produce. And after cooking and eating a meal with two or three different vegetables which less than an hour before had still been in the ground or on the stalks, I would say with some rather smug satisfaction, "the Queen cannot get fresher than that".

The plot next to us had at last been let to Frank and Sheila who had just moved into the new house nearest to our own plot. In conversation with L. one day Sheila said how much they would like to have our plot, as it was right next to their new house - just over the fence. What better than to offer it to them before it was advertised, and thus save the Parish Clerk the job of finding a new tenant? This arrangement was soon settled and Frank and Sheila would also buy our rotovator and grass cutter.

Later on, as the cropping season ended, the potato and bean haulms were cleared away for compost and the vegetables were packed and stored in sacks or blanched and frozen. Clearing out the sheds now became a necessity before we handed them over to the new tenants. This shed work produced a vast amount of burnable material, mostly wood, cardboard and paper, and we needed to have a bonfire two or three times a week. But here was a problem. The first of the new houses were ready for occupation and the first of the new owners took up residence. It was not long before there were complaints from the new householders about the allotment fires, and the smoke and smuts which were allegedly besmirching the washing hanging on the lines in the new gardens. So we were limited to lighting a fire only when the wind was blowing from the east or from the south when it would carry the smoke away from the new estate.

We had an enormous amount of compost in our bins and decided to take some of it home - having first ascertained that no hibernating animals were in it. It was much superior to the compost sold at the Co-op, and to Tesco's 'Grobags', and we bagged up about a dozen sacks for use in the garden at home.

CHAPTER SEVENTEEN

The shed clearance also showed us how many tools we had collected up. The best ones which we could use at home we kept. At one stage I counted seven trowels and five pairs of secateurs, three pairs of which were pretty useless. We offered everything we did not need to Matt, who took the nets, surplus wood, stepladders, a Briggs and Stratton mower and any of the chemicals which he could use. The bicycles kept in the pigsty now had to be brought out and housed somewhere at home until they were eventually disposed of.

In the middle of that winter Ted died unexpectedly. Ted, you will recall, was a plotholder who from time to time swopped experiences of Desert warfare with L., and who, with Matt, had helped me by covering our blackcurrant bushes with netting when L. was incapacitated. One of Ted's sons asked L. to look and see what was in his shed and to take anything we could find a use for. And would L. collect all the trays of seed potatoes from Ted's garage? L. had a word with Matt and together they looked in the shed. Unlike our own sheds there was very little in it and we certainly did not need anything from it. L. brought trays and trays of seed potatoes from Ted's garage and showed them to Matt who said they could be accommodated in his sheds and eventually he would distribute them around to the other plotholders.

We would all miss Ted. He was a familiar and well-respected figure on the gardens. We would miss seeing his tall, lean frame striding up and down the paths, his white hair blowing in the wind.

Some of us attended his funeral. The vicar in his address remarked, "I see that the allotments are nicely represented here", and told us more about Ted than we had ever learned from chatting to him on the gardens. And so we said 'goodbye' to him; his allotment-gardening days had come to an abrupt end.

CHAPTER EIGHTEEN

A nd now our own allotment-gardening days were about to end, though not with such absolute finality.

Over the past two or three years we had often discussed and speculated as to what would be the manner of our departure from the gardening scene. Then it seemed as though we would be driven out by the building firm. I particularly would have been devastated if this had happened. To have had to see the whole field developed and all the gardens bulldozed and destroyed would have been heartbreaking, and it was, for a time, a scenario which seemed highly likely. Due to our campaigning to save the site we had been partially successful and half the plots had been saved; there was thus still a small (and fairly tranquil) area left in the village.

During those last visits to the allotment before we handed over the shed keys I already felt that it no longer belonged to us. Strangely I was not sad, in fact it was rather a relief. The responsibility for all that needed doing to keep it in good shape had become too much and we would not have wanted to struggle on in a half-hearted manner, seeing the plot become more and more run down.

We now asked ourselves what would we do with all the time we thought that we would have on our hands? I had great plans for the garden at home, which even though it was quite small had become rather neglected, and I looked forward to re-vitalising sections of it.

Looking back though, it had been a wonderful twelve years. The fresh air and the exercise; the satisfaction of growing and harvesting our own crops; the incomparable taste of the fresh fruit and vegetables; the friendship and the generosity of our fellow plotholders; the peace and tranquillity of so many warm days. There had of course been plenty of cold, wet, miserable days when we stamped about the paths in our boots, thick trousers, anoraks, and woolly hats and gloves, trying to keep warm by digging, and then lighting a bonfire and standing around it. But each day there had been a richness in the tasks we were doing - whether it was spreading manure, digging out nettles and thistles, looking eagerly to see if the parsnips had at last germinated, picking the soft fruit, cutting the courgettes, gathering the beans or digging the first new potatoes. How I would miss all the produce, especially the raspberries.

It had all been so well worth all the effort and hard work we had put into it. There had been difficulties along the way but with stout help and our own determination we had managed to overcome most of them. We knew that it had to come to an end sometime but we had not been able to envisage how this would come about, and we were reluctant to make a final decision ourselves. As it was, the decision was made for us; and perhaps, after all, this was the best way for it to end.

EPILOGUE

You may wonder, reader, what happened after we gave up our allotment?

It was in fact not the end. L's health improved and three years on we are still able to trundle slowly down to the gardens. Here we have a three-metre strip on one of Matt's plots. Matt does all the hard work for us: he manures the ground, rotovates and rakes it ready for us to sow our beans, shallots, onions, salad crops, courgettes and a few mixed flowers, and in due course we harvest the produce.

L. has made a big rectangular box with a hinged lid and in it we store our tools. The box is positioned amongst the wild brambles and bushes up against the bank and is virtually out of sight. In a nearby galvanised dustbin with a rubber lid we keep small items, knives, secateurs and sharpening stone, marker sticks, lines and a supply of plastic carrier bags.

We are slow now and find that an hour working on the garden is all that we can manage, but we are still able to sow the seeds and to watch the plants grow. We can stroll around the plots and admire the efforts of our fellow gardeners. Some of our old friends have, like us, reluctantly had to give up their plots - Tom, Taffy and Ernest - but we are pleased to see younger and more energetic new gardeners taking their places.

In early summer we pick our broad beans and Matt invites us to gather his redcurrants and gooseberries, and this we do. And later on we pick our scarlet runners with the multi-coloured sweet peas entwined amongst them. We try to cut all the courgettes before they become marrows almost overnight, but we never manage to catch them all. Those which are hidden under the great prickly leaves and which escape our knife and grow large we cut and leave on the green path for anyone to take, and we rejoice that someone always does take them.

We sit on the seat with Matt and have a chat. We discuss the state of the vegetable growth; the state of the latest on-goings in the village; the state of the world. We hear the distant cries of children in the school playground, the occa-sional drone of traffic over the bridge, a helicopter over-head. But all this is inconsequential and passes us by. We lis-ten instead to the birds, and we absorb the sun, the quiet scene and the soothing rich scents all around us.

*   *   *

We have no plans to retire - at our age one does not plan much ahead - but we know that the time will surely come, probably sooner rather than later, when we will put away our tools and hand the strip back to Matt. And even then - when we can no longer work in the garden - it will be diffi-cult to sever our links completely; so that on a fine and warm day you may possibly see us down there, just looking at the gardens, to see that everything is all right.